Brian Moses spends much of his time presenting his poetry and percussion show in schools, libraries and theatres.

His Macmillan poetry books have sold more than a million copies. He has always been fascinated by the past and the lessons that the past can teach us, although he wishes it to be known that he does not have a direct link with ancient Egyptian history as he is not a descendant of the man with the long white cloak, flowing beard and tablets of stone.

Contact Brian via his website: www.brianmoses.co.uk, and check out his blog: brian-moses.blogspot.com

Roger Stevens is a children's author and poet who visits schools and festivals, performing and running workshops. He enjoys performing in libraries too. If he had a time machine he would travel back to ancient Egypt in order to read the precious scrolls and books in the Library at Alexandria, one of the wonders of the ancient world, before it was destroyed by fire.

Roger lives in Brighton and in a little town in France with his wife and their very shy dog, Jasper. Roger also runs the Poetry Zone, where children can publish their poems and find out more about the exciting

poetry: w

Essex

30130

D0892954

Other books by Brian Moses and Roger Stevens

100% Unofficial! Olympic Poems
Brian Moses and Roger Stevens

What Are We Fighting For?
New Poems about War
Brian Moses and Roger Stevens

The Truth About Teachers
*Hilarious rhymes by Paul Cookson, David Harmer,
Brian Moses and Roger Stevens*

BRIAN MOSES & ROGER STEVENS

1066

And Before That

ILLUSTRATED BY
ANDREW WIGHTMAN

MACMILLAN CHILDREN'S BOOKS

First published 2016 by Macmillan Children's Books
an imprint of Pan Macmillan
20 New Wharf Road, London N1 9RR
Associated companies throughout the world
www.panmacmillan.com

ISBN 978-1-4472-8394-2

Text copyright © Brian Moses and Roger Stevens 2016
Illustrations copyright © Andrew Wightman 2016

The right of Brian Moses, Roger Stevens and Andrew Wightman to be
identified as the poets and illustrator of this work has been asserted by
them in accordance with the Copyright, Designs and Patents Act 1988.

All rights reserved. No part of this publication may be reproduced,
stored in a retrieval system, or transmitted, in any form or by any means
(electronic, mechanical, photocopying, recording or otherwise),
without the prior written permission of the publisher.

Pan Macmillan does not have any control over, or any responsibility for,
any author or third-party websites referred to in or on this book.

1 3 5 7 9 8 6 4 2

A CIP catalogue record for this book is available from
the British Library.

Printed and bound by CPI Group (UK) Ltd, Croydon CR0 4YY

This book is sold subject to the condition that it shall not,
by way of trade or otherwise, be lent, resold, hired out,
or otherwise circulated without the publisher's prior consent
in any form of binding or cover other than that in which
it is published and without a similar condition including this
condition being imposed on the subsequent purchaser.

For everyone at Ore Academy in Hastings, where
I am their Celebrity Author/Patron of Reading
B.M.

For Sam, who loves history
R.S.

CONTENTS

VERY EARLY DAYS: STONE AGE

ANCIENT EGYPT

ANCIENT GREECE

ANCIENT ROME

AFTER THE ROMANS

ICE AND SNOW

Born into a world of ice and snow
Everywhere you look
Everywhere you go
Ice and snow
More ice, more snow
Born into a world of ice and snow

There is a garden, far, far away
The rumours say, the rumours say
Where the sun always shines
And butterflies play . . .
What are they?
What are they?

Now we stoke the fire
With our dwindling wood
Wrapped up in our deer hides
Eat the last of our food
How I dream of a garden
With no ice and no snow

STONE AGE

What does that look like?
Will we ever know?
Ice and snow,
Ice and snow,
We'll never know

Roger Stevens

There is evidence that when the last great Ice Age happened, the humans that survived lived in an area on Africa's southern coast, the only part of the world that remained habitable. Some people claim that this was the basis for the Garden of Eden story in the Bible. And indeed for similar stories told by other religions and in other civilizations.

STONE AGE

TWO MAMMOTH POEMS

1. Why?

Why was a mammoth called a mammoth
and not an 'enormous' or a 'colossal'?
And how did they know what to call it
when they discovered the very first fossil?

2. Fossil

Now, many years from the Ice Age
a fossilized piece of bone
helps us make sense of the mammoth
like an ancient text message in stone.

Brian Moses

Greetings from 1500 BCE! Srsly.

It's a bit of a mystery why creatures were given their names. How did scientists and archaeologists know what to call their discoveries? And, of course, there's a message in everything we find from the past.

WHAT IS THE USE OF THAT?

What's that?
It's a wheel?
What does it do?
It goes round
Round and round
Along the ground.
Well, what is the use of that?

What's that?
It's a clock.
What does it do?
Tells the time.
We've the sun, we've the moon
Got midnight, got noon
Well, what is the use of that?

STONE AGE

What's that?
It's writing.
What does it do?
It's exciting.
All these new ideas
It will all end in tears
Now I've had my say, and that's that.

Roger Stevens

The ancient Sumer civilization grew up around the meeting point of the Euphrates and Tigris rivers in Mesopotamia (now known as Iraq) around seven thousand years ago, because of its natural fertility. It is often called the 'cradle of civilization' – and some people say the Sumerians were the world's greatest inventors.

CAVE PAINTING

A mammoth hunt
on a cave wall.

Stick people holding spears,

painted with charcoal,
stained with berries.

A tribe's history
handed down.

And below the hunt
a handprint.

A child, maybe,
reaching up . . .

STONE AGE

One thought in his head
to make it clear . . .

'I was here,
I existed,
I lived,
I survived . . .

'And this smudge of paint
on a wall
will say it all.'

Brian Moses

*Handprints and hand stencils were left by cave dwellers of all ages,
including children.*

INVITATION TO A CAVE RAVE
(A found poem)

Uay san grm urgle garumfff
Heffa dargle com dewyda.
Crum volla gan gowda guwalla
em tay unta flappu skewyva.

Garada ugla simso sarra sku
jaavada gu galla em furtle.
Heffu slapta don wolka em fluga
em slata solata dum myrtle.

Hep greer oof flaffa san.

STONE AGE

Translation:

Hey, man, can you dig it?
There's a cave rave at ours tonight.
The old folk are off hunting mammoths
and they won't be back before light.

Bring some of that very berry juice
that makes us laugh and sway.
There'll be music on drum and horn
and we'll party till break of day.

Be here, or be nowhere, man.

Brian Moses

STONE AGE

THE GOOD OLD STONE AGE DAYS

I don't hold with this new-fangled 'Bronze Age'.
What's it good for, eh?
What's wrong with the good old Stone Age days?

What's wrong with eating woolly mammoths?
Nothing like a good chewy hunk of mammoth's brain.
All this modern eating-vegetables malarkey
And growing grapes for wine.
What's wrong with drinking water
Like we did in the good old Stone Age days?

Why do we have to smelt copper
And alloy it with tin to make bronze vessels?
It will make the gods angry, mark my words.
The potter's wheel? That's just a phase.
Let's drink from hand-fashioned clay pots again
Like we did in the good old Stone Age days.

And all this 'writing' nonsense.
What's wrong with daubing a few pictures on the
    cave walls?
What's the point of writing things down?
And don't get me started on building houses!
What's so bad about living in caves?
Why else would the gods make holes in the ground?
So we can live in them, that's why!
Bring back the good old Stone Age days.

STONE AGE

No, this so-called Bronze Age is not for me.
Whatever next? Organized warfare?
It will all end in tears.
Mark my words.
Astronomy? Mathematics? Centralized government?
It's just the latest craze.
I say, Bring back the good old Stone Age days.

Roger Stevens

FAMILY TREE

Homo habilis
What must your fellow primates have thought of you
Two million years ago
With your handyman tools
And hand-crafted weapons?
You were top of the tree
Until *Homo erectus* showed up

Yes, *Homo erectus*
Migrating out of Africa
Over a million years ago
Spreading through Asia, Austro-Indonesia
And Europe
With your ability to make fire and cook
You were the bee's knees
Until the emergence of *Homo sapiens*
And *Homo neanderthalensis*

Alas, Neanderthals
You were clever
But not, it seems, clever enough
We lost you twenty-five thousand years ago
To the ice and snow

STONE AGE

And so, here we are
Homo sapiens
With your cave-painting skills
Advanced coordination skills allowing you to sew
And sophisticated linguistic communication
Which would eventually result in two *Homo sapiens*
Writing this book of poems

Roger Stevens

BURIAL MOUND

Long ago our ancestors
dug a ditch and raised a mound,
some Bronze Age barrow –
the resting place of a chieftain.
Part of the mound is hollowed out
and today children play there.

They put their ears to the ground
and listen to the rumble-belly
of a fallen warrior
deep within the mound.
They hear the battle cries that rang
across the hillside,
the clash of sword on sword,
the anger and the screams,
the history beneath their feet.

'And sometimes,' their teacher tells them,
'such chieftains were buried with a boat.'

'A boat.' Cries of disbelief.
'Where would he float to
in a boat?'

STONE AGE

'They thought,' their teacher replies,
'it would glide
from this world to the next –
over water, across the heavens.
Beyond the world we stand upon.'

And the children lie and listen
one more time,
for the flap of sail,
for the lap of waves,
for the echo from
a world unknown.

Brian Moses

A boat burial is where an important figure in the tribe was buried within a ship along with the usual grave goods such as weapons, food, jewellery and trinkets.

STONEHENGE

I remember Stonehenge
in the days when you could still
get close to the stones.
I remember being there, seeing their bulk
and feeling their solid substance.
It was the past brought close.
I could hear the tick of time,
the heartbeat of history.

If only the stones were transmitters,
they could broadcast their story,
answer the 'whys' of Stonehenge,
why Salisbury Plain gained
such a monument, why it was built –
was it temple or tomb?

It only we could summon solutions
from the sky, the clouds, the hills,
from those witnesses to the march
of these monoliths, to their positioning
and their raising.

And if only we knew who built this circle,
who mourned the winter sun
as the solstice darkened the day.
Did they ever imagine the puzzle
they were leaving behind?

STONE AGE

And I wonder again at the thread
between present and past,
at all those who have stood
by these stones, hoping to hear
some sort of message
to the living from the dead,
so one of history's mysteries
might be solved at last.

Brian Moses

Stonehenge was constructed when there were no written records so nobody really knows the answers to its mysteries – why it's where it is, what it was for, how the stones were transported such vast distances. All we really know is that it was of great importance in the past, and that it could be some kind of burial site.

THE PEASANT FARMER'S TALE

Each year upon the flooding of the Nile
I answer King Khufu's royal command
To work upon the building of his pyramid
The tallest structure ever built by hand

We've moved two million blocks of stone
And every one we've had to cut just right
Two elephants, that's fifteen tons in weight
No wonder that I'm shattered every night

For twenty years at Giza we have toiled
The wife says we should move, make a fresh start
But this I know will be a wonder of the world
And I feel honoured to have played my part

Roger Stevens

SHOE THE BLUES AWAY

A little-known fact
When King Tut had the blues
He'd wear one of his hundred
Pairs of shoes

Roger Stevens

THE NILE FLOOD

Hail to thee, O Nile,
and praise your wondrous flood,
the water that bursts your banks
to leave such fertile mud.

Where would we be without
your annual inundation?
How could we plant our crops
and ensure their cultivation?

Why you flooded was a mystery
only Hapi, the Nile god, knew.
Was it tears from Isis for Osiris?*
Many believed that was true.

 ANCIENT EGYPT

No one knew about monsoons
in the mountains of the south,
unleashing torrents of water
that rolled to your mighty mouth.

Too little rain would cause famine,
too much would wash houses away.
Just enough would leave behind
the fertile mud and clay.

So hail to thee, O Nile,
and praise your wondrous flood.
For those of us beside you,
your water is our lifeblood.

Brian Moses

*Ancient Egyptians believed that the Nile flooded every year because of Isis's tears of sorrow for her dead husband, Osiris.

THE CURSE OF OSIRIS

A million suns
Had blazed across the sky,
A million moons
Had bathed the shifting sands
With their reflected light,
As deep beneath the pyramid
The young King Tutankhamun
Dreamed of stars that shone
Upon an endless night.

When Lord Carnarvon,
Howard Carter and their crew
Discovered Tutankhamun's tomb
They little did suspect
That, by disturbing Tutankhamun's rest,
They would release the Curse of Osiris
To dog their every step.

A snake ingested Carter's pet canary
And then each day an accident or some
Strange death. And five months on
The cursed Carnarvon died and, it is said,
His faithful terrier, in England, far away,
Howled to the moon and also dropped down dead.

Coincidence?
You may be right.
But tell me why the lights of Cairo all went out
Upon that fateful night?

Roger Stevens

22 ANCIENT EGYPT

YOU CAN'T TAKE IT WITH YOU WHEN YOU GO, OR CAN YOU?

It seems the pharaohs thought that you could,
and there was more than just a likelihood

that possessions they'd collected before they died
might be useful to them on the other side.

Sharpened swords with which to fight
their enemies in the long dark night.

A slave girl, comely, to serve them food
and administer to their every mood.

Amulets with spells to overpower
evil forces in their weakest hour.

Dogs and cats now mummified
to keep them company when they died.

And Kha their pyramid
    architect who
was buried with his portaloo!*

Brian Moses

*It's true! The pyramid architect Kha
who designed royal tombs was actually
buried with his own portable toilet!*

THE AFTERLIFE

So, Osiris, please tell me
What happens when I die?

**First, mortal,
you must persuade the ferryman
to ferry you across
the river of death**

And if I manage that?

**Then you must pass through
The Twelve Gates
Each guarded
by a ferocious serpent**

Twelve gates?
Sounds tricky.
But if I make it?

ANCIENT EGYPT

Your third ordeal will be to cross
The blazing Lake of Fire
Where you will be judged

Oh, I see.
And if by chance
I've led a blameless life?

Why, you will live forever
And your soul
Will travel through
The heavens

But what if I have sinned?

Ha! Then you
will be fed to the monster!

I think we may as well
get it over with.
Just feed me to the monster now

Roger Stevens

THE GREAT PYRAMID

Legend tells that Napoleon Bonaparte
once spent a night alone
inside the Great Pyramid.

Something happened that night,
but, whatever it was, he never told,
never spoke of what he witnessed.
He took the secret to his grave.

'To him that toucheth the tomb
of the pharaoh,' it was written,
'death will come on soft wings.'*

All I know is that nothing would induce me
to tempt the past, to spend a night
in a pyramid, to lift a lid,
unwrap a mummy
and inhale its breath . . .

 ANCIENT EGYPT

(Or to sneak into tombs
on the Theban west bank
and be frightened to bits
by the mummy pits.)

Brian Moses

From an Arab text

There were many curses and superstitions attached to pyramids and tombs to deter thieves from breaking in. The mummy pits were mass burials of mummies in huge numbers.

TOOTHACHE

I've tried the usual things to drive away
The fenet worm
Which gnaws upon my tooth
Rotton vegetables and horse manure
The sacred Nile's mud and jackal's blood
But frankly
None have been much use

O Ma'at,
Goddess of justice and of truth,
my tooth's in agony
I cannot stand the pain
What did I do to upset you so?
I swear by Amun's crown
I'll not do it again

Roger Stevens

In ancient Egypt the fenet worm was thought to be the cause of many ailments and diseases – such as toothache.

ANCIENT EGYPT

THE WEIRDEST EXHIBIT

The museum galleries
go on for miles;
you see furniture and furnishings,
tapestries and tiles.
You see kitchens where fire grates
are blackened with soot,
but the weirdest exhibit
is a mummified foot.

It's gruesome and gross
but you'll love it the most,
the Egyptian mummified foot.

You can see right inside
where the skin has been ripped,
then you'll notice the bone
and the way it's been chipped.
And beneath the bandage
you'll see actual flesh . . .
I bet it smelt cheesy
even when it was fresh!

It's gruesome and gross
but you'll love it the most,
the Egyptian mummified foot.

And what's so amazing,
what's really fantastic:
the toenails are real
and not made of plastic.
And beneath the nails
you can see grains of sand.
Are they picked at each night
by a mummified hand?

It's gruesome and gross
but you'll love it the most,
the Egyptian mummified foot.

Brian Moses

*A few years ago when I visited the Cheltenham Art Gallery & Museum
I found an Egyptian mummified foot on display. It may still be there.*

ANCIENT EGYPT

THREE ANCIENT GREEKS

1
He laid the foundations of Western
    science and philosophy
He was one hot potato
His ideas reached escape
    velocity
They called him Plato

2
He discussed the theory of the soul
He introduced the golden mean
Because of him we can use logic
His writing was a dream
Ethics, aesthetics, politics
Linguistics, rhetoric too
Theatre, poetry, government
What couldn't this man do?
He was like an express train
Racing at full throttle
He was history's first true scientist
And his name was Aristotle

3
His empire stretched from Greece
  to the North of India
As rulers go, he was a
  heavyweight
He was King of Macedonia,
  Pharaoh of Egypt, King of
  Persia and King of Asia
No wonder they called him
  Alexander the Great

Roger Stevens

Aristotle was a student of Plato. And Alexander the Great was a student
of Aristotle.

 ANCIENT GREECE

IF I WAS . . .

If I was as moody as Poseidon
no one would dare to approach me.

If I was as gloomy as Hades
I could darken a room with my presence.

If I was as speedy as Hermes
I would be a gold medallist
in every Olympic Games.

If I was as wise as Athena
I would know the answers to questions
before they were asked.

If I was as strong as Hercules
I could lift the weight of worries
from everyone's shoulders.

If I was as beautiful as Aphrodite
I would shine like a star
in the darkest of nights.

If I was as noisy as Zeus
I would hear my voice thunder
in every sentence I spoke.

But if I had the heel of Achilles
I'd be careful, very careful indeed.

Brian Moses

The Greek gods all had different responsibilities and were often known for their good or bad qualities. Achilles was a Greek warrior who, when still a baby, was dipped in the River Styx by his mother Thetis to make him invulnerable. As she held on to his heel while she dipped him, that spot was never covered and remained his weak spot. Today, if someone has a weakness, it is often known as their 'Achilles heel'.

 ANCIENT GREECE

DIOGENES (1)

(A pantoum)

I've no use for a house, you see
No table, no chairs and no bed
I don't need a palace of finely cut stone
Or even an old timbered shed

No table, no chairs and no bed
I never have friends round to dine
My home is a jar with room for just me
And it's based on the snail's design

I never have friends round to dine
A barrel's not roomy in truth
Though the top can be used as a table
If you like to eat from the roof

A barrel's not roomy in truth
I've no use for a house, you see
We come into this world with nothing
And nothing's enough for me

Roger Stevens

DIOGENES (2)

Bit of a squeeze for Diogenes
inside his pottery jar.

Wedged in tight, snail-like,
he couldn't move very far.

Couldn't walk from room to room
or plan any DIY.

Couldn't pop down to the shops
and seek out furniture to buy.

Couldn't invite a friend to stay
and say there's plenty of space.

ANCIENT GREECE

Couldn't say, just step inside
while I take care of your case.

And didn't you freeze, Diogenes,
in the winter without any heat?

And didn't people think you were crazy
when they passed you on the street?

And what did you do in the middle of the night
when you needed to use the loo?

Sounds crazy to me, Diogenes,
I'm glad I'm me and not you.

Brian Moses

*Diogenes was a Greek philosopher who lived in Athens from 400 to 325 BCE.
He preached austerity and begged for a living. He slept in a large pottery jar
in the market place in Athens.*

*Alexander the Great is said to have met Diogenes and asked him if, given his
great power and wealth, there was anything he could do for him. Diogenes
said, 'Yes, please move over. You're blocking my sun.'*

ARCHIMEDES

Sure, if you need to measure
A circle, or a cylinder or a sphere
Archimedes is your man

Or if you need an ingenious pump
That can raise water uphill
To irrigate your vines
Archimedes is your guy

And when he climbed into the bath
And realized that you could figure the volume
Of irregular objects
From their displacement of water
Pure genius!
(Although some would say
Jumping out of the bath
Running down the street naked
Shouting Eureka! I have found it!
Was a little – how shall we say? –
Theatrical)

 ANCIENT GREECE

But his plan to construct a ray gun
By building giant mirrors
To concentrate beams of light
To set ships on fire?
And his plan to build a giant crane
To lift enemy ships
Out of the water
And shake them in mid-air?
Just a little . . . what . . .
Over the top?

Still, I suppose we have to give these creative types
The benefit of the doubt.
And Archimedes' pump IS very useful

Roger Stevens

Archimedes (287–c.212 BCE) is generally considered to be one of the leading scientists and mathematicians of all time. He discovered how to work out the area of a circle and the volume of a sphere. And he is credited with designing innovative machines such as the screw pump, compound pulleys and war machines to protect his native Syracuse from invasion.

THE SUBURBS OF OLYMPUS

We wanted to be near the gods
so we moved to the suburbs of Olympus,
but these gods are the neighbours from Hades
and their noise is too much for us.

Zeus always loses his temper,
and we're tired of hearing him swear.
But worst of all is when he hurls
mighty thunderbolts through the air.

In the daytime they knock us off our feet,
at night we're rocked from our beds.
Our nerves are shattered, our senses battered,
these thunderbolts fill us with dread.

Just as bad is his brother Poseidon
whose voice is loud and strident.
Like Zeus, his orders reverberate
as he shakes the world with his trident.

And each dawn we hear Apollo's
horse-drawn chariot bustling by,
on its course to position the sun
in its place against the sky.

Apollo can view the future
and so people flock to his side,
forming noisy queues and calling
for him to be their guide.

The armourer of the gods
is Hephaestus, the god of fire.
We hear him forging swords
in the heat of a crackling pyre.

Most nights the gods hold parties
that resound around Olympus.
How I wish we'd never moved here now,
the suburbs are not for us.

Brian Moses

*This poem imagines that the Greek gods on Mount Olympus were a noisy
bunch and that anyone living close to the mountain would be disturbed by
their behaviour.*

A GIFT FROM THE GREEKS

Praise the gods
The siege is lifted
Rejoice
And see
A wooden horse

It is huge
I doubt we'll hardly
Haul it through our gates

They say
It is dedicated to their god, Athena
To grant them safe passage home
Laocoön suspects some trickery involved
I fear the Greeks, he says
Even bearing gifts

But no,
We will bring it into the city
Despite its great size
It will be our Victory Trophy
And the celebrations
Will go on
Far into the night . . .

Roger Stevens

The horse was pulled into the city, but the Trojans were unaware that it was full of Greek soldiers. That night the soldiers came out, opened the gates for the returned army and Troy fell. No one knows if this story is true.

 ANCIENT GREECE

IT'S CALLED MONEY

What's this?
It's a coin.
Are you joking?
I've given you half a sack of grain.
And I've given you a coin.
It's just a scrap of metal.
It's electrum.
Are you pulling my leg?
I've given you half a sack of the very best quality
barley.
Look, the coin's stamped with an ear of barley.
But I've given you real *barley!*
Sorry, but I haven't got any cloth left.
Tell you what, I'll give you two coins.
You're having a laugh!
Two coins and you can borrow
My best-laying chicken for a week.
Now you're talking.
It's a deal!

Roger Stevens

Coins were introduced as a method
of payment around the sixth or fifth
century BCE. The invention of coins is
still shrouded in mystery: according
to Herodotus, coins were first minted
by the Lydians, while Aristotle
claims that the first coins were
minted by the wife of King Midas of
Phrygia. Numismatists consider that
the first coins were minted on the
Greek island of Aegina.

ANCIENT GREECE

MEANWHILE, TWO AND A HALF THOUSAND YEARS AGO, BENEATH THE MAJESTIC MOUNTAINS OF THE INDIAN HIMALAYAS . . .

Under cover of darkness
in the silence of the night
the young prince Siddhārtha
left the riches of the palace
to seek the meaning of life
to understand why all creatures suffer
to understand how to escape from suffering
and his life as a monk began

And many, many years later
he finally understood
that good deeds lead the way
that suffering arises from greed
which in turn arises from thinking
that we are more important than everybody else
He saw how beings are reborn
according to the law of cause and effect, or karma
And thus Siddhārtha became the Buddha,
the Supreme Enlightened One,
and Buddhism began

Roger Stevens

TIME FOR A CHOCOLATE DRINK, I THINK

Chocolate
I'm loving it
I've harvested
Some cacao beans
I'm going to make
A chocolate drink
Fermented them
And dried them too
I've roasted them
Removed their shells
And ground them
To a silky paste
With water
And a little love
Some cornmeal
For consistency
And chilli
For a little heat
Some cinnamon
That yummy taste
Just can't be beat
It looks a treat
Then shake it up

That's just enough
And pour from one cup
To the next
And back and forth
To make some froth
That looks brilliant
Whaddya think?
Would you like to share my
Chocolate drink?

Roger Stevens

The first chocolate beverage is believed to have been created by the Mayan civilization around 2,000 years ago. The chocolate drink was also used in religious ceremonies and exchanged between bride and groom during the traditional marriage ceremony.

ROMULUS AND REMUS

Do you remember our mum?
How we snuggled deep
Into her winter coat, so warm
In summer chased her tail
And played in the forest that was home?

Who could imagine now
That foundlings such as we
Could found an empire
Such as Rome

Roger Stevens

JULIUS CAESAR'S LAST BREAKFAST

I'm tired this morning, off my food
Hardly touched the olives, lark or dormouse
We stayed out late last night with Lepidus
And talked of death
Drank too much wine
And now Calpurnia, my wife, is in a mood
She dreamed a death
And it was mine

I'm tired this morning
The winds of March
Are blowing like a hurricane through Rome
At the Pontifical Palace
The God of Mars crashed to the floor
And what that means I'm not quite sure

ANCIENT ROME

I'm tired this morning
Upon the Ides of March
The Senate can convene without me
Yes, I think I'll stay at home

Roger Stevens

On the morning of Julius Caesar's assassination, the chamber at the Senate was full. But Caesar's chair was empty. He was nowhere to be found. The conspirators sent Marcus Brutus to Caesar's house to persuade him to attend.

WOAD

Let's all go out
and plaster ourselves with woad
(yeah woad!),
frighten everybody silly
as we stomp down the Roman road
(in woad!).

Once we've covered ourselves
with woad,
we'll look twice as ugly
as a warty toad
in woad
(yeah woad!).

We're walking down the Roman road
wearing woad.
Walking down the Roman road
wearing woad.

Woad is great,
woad is cool.
Woad will defeat
the Roman rule.

Woad will help us all
to survive
rushing chariot queues
on the M XXV.

 ANCIENT ROME

We're walking down the Roman road
wearing woad.
Walking down the Roman road
wearing woad.

Saw ourselves in the lake
and nearly died.
You haven't lived
if you haven't tried
WOAD!
(Yeah woad!)

The fashion accessory
of the Iron Age.

Brian Moses

'All the Britons dye their bodies with woad, which produces a blue colour,
and this gives them a more terrifying appearance in battle' Julius Caesar

THE VINDOLANDA RUN

In winter, instead of Roman feet
tramping the iron frost fields,
soldiers slid slalom-like over snow,
riding on upturned shields.

It was wonderful fun – the Romans could think
of nothing that they enjoyed more,
a toboggan run down Cuddy's Crag,
much better than going to war!

And fresh recruits would think it easy
as off on their shields they flew,
till they'd hit a rock and topple off
and the moorland air would turn blue

with Latin oaths and curses they flung
at an unsympathetic sky –
then they'd dust themselves off and climb back up
to the top for another try.

In the ice and snow it was all systems go
for the soldiers patrolling the wall,
they'd challenge each other to see who could travel
the longest without a fall.

ANCIENT ROME

Reputations were made or lost
on a run that went really well.
From around the Empire soldiers would beg
for a post at this once northern hell.

And no one thought of war any more;
Pict bashing had had its day.
The Romans were far too busy
inviting their enemies round to play!

Brian Moses

*Vindolanda was a busy Roman fort close to Hadrian's Wall.
Roman soldiers were stationed there first for long periods of time and must
have got quite bored. This poem imagines one way in which they might have
had some fun in their spare time.*

BOUDICCA IS COMING TO TOWN
(After *'Santa Claus is Coming to Town'*)

You'd better not fight,
you'd better retreat.
Get out of the kitchen
if you can't stand the heat.
Boudicca is coming to town.

She's seeking revenge,
to even the score.
She'll find where you're hid
and knock down your door.
Boudicca is coming to town.

She won't be taking prisoners,
she's out to win or die.
She's routed Roman legions
with her fearsome battle cry.

You'd better not fight,
you'd better retreat.
Get out of the kitchen
if you can't stand the heat.
Boudicca is coming to town.

Londinium's in lockdown,
there's chaos everywhere.
The Romans know this she-devil
will drive them to despair.

You'd better not fight,
you'd better retreat.
Get out of the kitchen
if you can't stand the heat.
Boudicca is coming to town.

Brian Moses

Boudicca, Queen of the Iceni tribe in Roman Britain, led an uprising against the Romans. She captured Colchester, which was then the capital of Roman Britain, and moved on to take London. Thousands were killed in the uprising until Boudicca was finally defeated by the Romans.

EQUUS

The Emperor Caligula was mad
Of course.
To help him rule he promoted to the Senate
His horse

The horse was good and just but rather negative
Or so they say
In big debates the horse would always answer
Neigh!

Roger Stevens

'Equus' is Latin for horse.

ELEPHANT TEARS

There was no idea of ecology
in ancient Rome, no sense of awe
or wonder at creatures unknown.
It was a nightly feast of
kill or be killed, man against beast,
lion against tiger, till finally
elephants were prodded into elevators
and raised to the floor of the Colosseum
to be gifted to the arena.

And already the ground was stained
by the blood of so many
slain creatures,
but only the elephants extracted
any kind of pity
from those who came
to catch the carnage.
Maybe the tears in elephant eyes
and the sound of their lamentations
echoed the crowd's unease
at the enjoyment of such slaying.

But their emperor approved,
and knew, of course,
about living by the sword.
His word was law, and to pretend
otherwise was foolish.
And there had been
so many emperors, fifteen
in forty years.
Less sympathy surely for them
than for those elephant tears.

Brian Moses

Many thousands of wild animals were brought to the Colosseum to be killed in front of watching crowds. Even the most hard-hearted in the audience were sometimes moved by the sight of elephants' tears.

A SHOW IN THE COLOSSEUM

The lion leaped, I dodged, I danced,
I struck the creature with my lance.
His claw drew blood.
I winced, I cried,
I held my side.
He leaped again, I dodged, I ducked
I threw my net and caught his mane
And with my lance
I cancelled out my debt.
The lion died.

I heard the crowd roar,
Cheer, applaud.
I looked to Caesar, saw him frown
His hand extended
Thumb held . . .

(Or if you prefer a happy ending . . .)

I looked as Caesar raised his cup
Of wine. He smiled,
His thumb held . . .

Roger Stevens

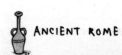 ANCIENT ROME

READING THE ENTRAILS

The priest pulled
From the dead sheep's body
Its blood-soaked intestine
And proclaimed

The sun will shine upon
Your son and daughter
The clouds will rain
Upon your vines and crops

(Excuse me,
Now I need
Some soap and water.

Lots.)

Roger Stevens

TORTOISE

The skills we learned from our forbears
and all the tactics they taught us,
do nothing now and cannot resist
the advance of the Roman tortoise.

Shields interlock to form a roof
that covers each soldier's back,
while those at the front form a barrier
as the army begins to attack.

Arrows bounce off uselessly
as the tortoise lumbers along.
Spears can't pierce its armour;
the shell is far too strong.

  ANCIENT ROME

So strong that men could walk on it,
or drive chariots over its back,
something they do in training to check
that it won't collapse or crack.

And it can't be turned upside down
like a real one can turn roly-poly.
The tortoise presses on through,
surely . . . but slowly.

Brian Moses

In battle the Romans carried rectangular curved shields made of wood and
leather, then plated with iron or bronze. Soldiers interlocked their shields
and crouched beneath them. Then they advanced against the enemy in a
method of attack known as the tortoise.

ROMAN CURSES

Romans, it seems, were easily aroused
to cast curses on others, like evil spells
written in clay and left to be found
at baths or shrines or holy wells.

Docimedis wrote at the baths in Bath
that a thief should lose both his eyes and mind
for stealing a pair of his favourite gloves,
and nobody thought him unkind.

Biccus prayed that his enemy would suffer
both insomnia and constipation,
and for the theft of a towel this thief
lived in fear and trepidation.

Experts would be paid to write curses
so they wouldn't misfire or fail.
Debtors might be told they should pay in blood
or else spend time in jail.

Punishment was handed over to gods
who were often called upon to choose
the guilty one from a list of suspects
and decide whose property was whose.

Everyone, it seems, wanted revenge
with no one willing to forgive.
Would we have been different ourselves,
more willing to live and let live?

I doubt it when I see sometimes
what's written on Facebook or Twitter.
Romans, it seems, are among us still
and their curses are just as bitter.

Brian Moses

*Roman curses were written in clay. There are a number on display in the
museum attached to the Roman Baths in Bath.*

ODE TO A ROMAN ROAD
(After Horace 65–8 BCE and Keats 1795–1821)

O magnificent road, how straight thou art,
Not a bend, a curve, a hill or a tree
To distract either chariot or cart
From purposeful and needful journey,
Where soldiers would march without fuss or fear
And rest from foot-slogging on grassy banks.
Commanders could see for miles around
Foes who were drawing near
And legions were readied in solid ranks,
While orders were given to stand iron-bound.*

ANCIENT ROME

O road, you'll be remembered through history,
The skills of your builders will be acclaimed.
Many will marvel at the mystery
Of how rough and rugged landscape was tamed
By those who laboured with shovel and pick
To connect each town like links in a chain.
A pattern was laid and so to this day
Our own roads often stick
Closely to those of the Roman terrain.
Let's recognize those who showed us the way.

Brian Moses

* *iron-bound means unyielding*

An ode is written in praise of something.

JESUS – THE TRUTH

It's hard to find
Hard evidence
That Jesus was real
So much was written about Him
So long after He died
But we do know
The effect these writings
Have had on the world
Now two billion Christians
Celebrate His resurrection from the dead
On Easter day
And I like to think
About His message in the Bible
That we should love one another
And love our enemies as ourselves
And I think
Should we really be fighting wars
In His name?

Roger Stevens

ANCIENT ROME

DON'T PICK A FIGHT WITH A PICT

The Roman Army has issued an edict:
don't pick a fight with a Pict.
Don't call out names to his sister or brother,
whatever you do, don't bad-mouth his mother.

It isn't worth all the aggro and fuss,
a Pict will never be one of us.
He's a fearsome figure, his body tattooed,
the Pictish nation will not be subdued.

If they stay where they are they're no trouble at all,
we don't want them swarming over the wall,
these savages with hair on their faces
and few clothes to cover important places.

If we watch them closely, we'll see what they're doing
and prevent our wall from becoming a ruin.
So obey these orders and cease any conflict:
don't pick a fight with a Pict.

Brian Moses

Picts were a Scottish tribe during and after the Roman occupation.
Gildas was a sixth-century monk who recounted the story of Britain before
and after the Saxons came. He called Picts 'marauding savages' and said
they had more hair on their faces than they had clothes on their bodies.

TO BE A DRUID YOU NEED TO . . .

Have a well-stocked memory,
learn a whole heap of poetry.

Remember strange formulae,
interpret secrets in the sky.

Memorize tribal history,
know all about magic and mystery.

Be free of sins and vices,
carry out human sacrifices.

Spend twenty years, at least,
learning to be a priest.

Now, who wants to be a Druid?

Not me!

Brian Moses

Training to be a druid was a lengthy
and rigorous undertaking, requiring
great dedication.

ANCIENT ROME

THE BONES OF YOU

I'm looking at the bones of you
and wishing I knew who you were.
Female, they say, third-century CE,
and wealthy too, they deduce,
from the scallop shell on your coffin.
Daughter, maybe, of some rich
Roman merchant.

Perhaps he showed you off at banquets,
hoping for a noble match.
Quite a catch, I suspect:
narrow waist, slender hips.
Maybe you paraded the room,
designer label on your toga,
fine hands, skin untroubled by
housework or cooking, serving food
to your father's business clients.

Now the grave goods they buried
alongside your body give us further clues
to who you were, the perfumed oils,
the hairpins, the jet.
It's the pull of history
and it's fascinating
looking at the bones of you,
tying up the known and the unknown.

Brian Moses

In one line of this poem there is an anachronism – an object in its wrong time. Can you spot it? Archaeology is all about tying up the known and the unknown in the hope that something near the truth will emerge.

 ANCIENT ROME

UNFAMILIAR TONGUES

'The British sealed their doom by inviting them [invaders] in among them, like wolves in the sheep fold' Gildas

We shouldn't have spent
so much time
applauding marauding bands.

It was our fault,
we welcomed them in,
only to discover
they were wolves
in our sheep pen.

Time and again they came,
speaking in unfamiliar tongues.

Their language
the thrust of a spear.

AFTER THE ROMANS

Their greeting
the swing of an axe.

We should have learned
after so many attacks.

We should have
seen the sails, turned tail
and run.

Or hidden in ambush,
the advantage ours.

We were too trusting,
ready to shake hands,
to divvy up the land
and live peacefully.

But they were bent on
busting our heads,
pinning skulls to their doorposts.

And again and again
we didn't learn,
and again and again
they returned.

Brian Moses

Invasions happened time and time again after the Romans left. Initially the Brits were welcoming but slowly began to realize that all the invaders were hostile.

 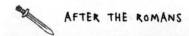 AFTER THE ROMANS

WE ARE THE ANGLO SAXONS

We are the Anglo Saxons
Anglo Saxons all
Cos we hate the Romans
We hate the Romans
How we love to see the Romans fall

We're a little bit of Jute
From Germany
A little bit of Saxon can be found
A little bit of Friesian
From the Netherlands
And the locals, of course, are still around
A few sea wolves from the darkest north
(Although we're not sure if they're friends or foe)
We've a few wodenists who worship the Earth
And we thought you might like to know
That . . .

We are the Anglo Saxons
Anglo Saxons all
Cos we hate the Romans
We hate the Romans
How we love to see the Romans fall

We've been under their thumb
For far too long
Four hundred years of Roman subjugation
Now we don't have to wash
And all of that tosh
It's goodbye to the Roman nation
We burnt down their palace at Fishbourne
Winchester we levelled to the ground
And if you're looking for
The Roman City of Eagles
Well, it can no longer be found
Because . . .

We are the Anglo Saxons
Anglo Saxons all
Cos we hate the Romans
We hate the Romans
How we love to see the Romans fall

Roger Stevens

 AFTER THE ROMANS

ADVICE TO A VIKING GIRL FROM HER PARENTS

Don't tell me that Harald Bloodbath
is the man that you adore.
His manners are nil, his attitude mean
and he's such a dreadful bore.

All Harald wants to talk about
are the warriors that he's slain.
What seems to give him pleasure
is giving others pain.

Don't tell me that he's the man
that you are intending to marry?
There must surely be a more courteous
Tom or Dick or Harry?

Harald is not the man
we would choose for a son-in-law.
His life just seems to revolve
around blood and guts and gore.

Every dispute is resolved
with an axe he calls 'skull-breaker'
and a double handed sword
he's nicknamed 'widow-maker'.

He's selfish and he's sly
and we worry he will do you harm.
His very name, 'Bloodbath',
fills us with fear and alarm.

There must be someone else
among the Viking nobility,
someone with charm and manners
who can offer you more stability.

Eric the Quiet, Ivor the Pious,
both sound like they would do.
So won't you tell Harald Bloodbath
he's not the man for you?

Brian Moses

Parents then would have been just as worried about their children as
they are today. Families would have always wanted good marriages for
their sons and daughters.

THE TRUTH ABOUT VIKINGS

Well, Mr Walton. Do you like my story?
About the Vikings and how they would fight?
Indeed I do, young Roger Magoo
But you haven't quite got your facts right
Do you like my description of their helmets with
    horns?
That they wore on each mad Viking raid?
Indeed I do, Young Roger Magoo
But their helmets were hornless, I'm afraid
Well, my Vikings don't wash, and they're stinky to
    boot
Like the way smelly socks start to reek
Well, they used tweezers, and combs, and razors to
    shave
And they bathed in hot springs once a week
Yes, but we all know that Vikings were callous and
    cruel
As they raided the land from their boats
A few, that is true, but most farmed the land
Sowing grain, raising pigs, sheep and goats
They treated their women abominably
And that was the Vikings' vile boast
No, women could inherit, they could get a divorce
In fact they had more freedom than most
Anyway, Mr Walton, do you like my account
Despite the few things I got wrong?

Indeed I do, young Roger Magoo
The story just swept me along
For the telling of tales is what counts in the end
But in tales you do need a twist
Those chieftain-led tribes used to fight, and back then
The term Viking . . . well, it didn't exist

Roger Stevens

Once upon a time, a long time ago, I wrote a book of poems with Celia Warren called Vikings Don't Wear Pants. *We launched the book at the Viking Museum in York. It was there that a 'Viking' told me I'd got the poem wrong. Vikings did wear pants. Which is why I've written this poem.*

AFTER THE ROMANS

RADGAR HAIRY BREECHES

You might think that someone with a name like
Radgar Hairy Breeches
would be a bit of a joke.
Well, you'd be wrong.

He was a fierce Viking warrior,
brave and strong.
Radgar would fight anyone
and win.

In any Viking football team
he'd have been the one that everyone bid for.
He'd be an astronomical sum
on the transfer sheet.

Those who didn't know him
would burst out laughing when they heard his name.
But it would be the last thing they did
before he cut them down.

He led a furious army
in blitzkrieg attacks.
He was a battering ram
of a man.

Radgar Hairy Breeches,
Radgar shaggy trousers.

His sons too had strange names:
Sigurd Snake-in-the-Eye,
Ivar the Boneless.

Wonder if they ever wished for
ordinary names,
names like Brian
or Roger.

Brian Moses

Today we think that some of the names given to Vikings were very strange indeed.

 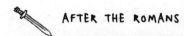 AFTER THE ROMANS

SKÖFNUNG

My name is Sköfnung
and I was buried beside King Hrólfr
after a long and bloody battle
Skeggi Bjarnason, the thief
broke into the king's burial mound and stole me
and took me across the sea to Iceland
There Skeggi's son, Eiðr, inherited me
and gave me on loan to Þorkell Eyjólfsson
to avenge the death of his son.
Much later I was with Þorkell on a ship carrying timber
A squall capsized us and all aboard were drowned
but I was washed up on an island in the fjord.
Gellir found me and on we travelled to Norway,
to distant Rome, and then to Denmark,
where Gellir died and was buried.

Where am I now? Nobody knows.
And this is my story, told in Viking sagas handed down
across five centuries.

Who am I?
I am Sköfnung

What am I?
Do you know?

Roger Stevens

TO THE RIM OF THE WORLD
(A poem for two voices)

When will we sail
in our dragon boat?

When will we sail?

When the day is lucky,
when the gods decide,

that's when we'll sail.

Who will come with us
across the waves?

Who will come with us?

Heroes and warriors
brave and strong,

that's who'll come.

What will we take
on our epic voyage?

What will we take?

We'll take our courage
and the sharpest of swords,

that's what we'll take.

  AFTER THE ROMANS

And where will we go
in this watery world?

Where will we go?

*The gods will show us
where to row,*

that's where we'll go.

And what will we find
at the rim of the world?

What will we find?

*Who knows, my friend,
who knows . . .*

Brian Moses

There was huge speculation in Viking times about what might lie at the edge of the world. Nobody knew that the world was round and sailors were scared of what they might find when they sailed to the edge.

EIGHT SWORDS

Death Bringer
Fear Striker
Starlight Catcher
Body Halver
Blood Letter
Mercy Killer
Head Splitter
Flesh Carver

Roger Stevens

Vikings used to give their swords names. Maybe along the lines of this kenning. There was once a famous sword called Sköfnung.

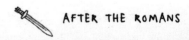

KING CANUTE

Once more on to the beach, dear friends, once more
And fill our boots up with this English sand
You say I am a god? That I could command
The sea itself to back away from me? Let's see –
And make today a day that no one will forget!

He tried. He failed.
And everyone got wet.

Roger Stevens

Canute invaded England and became king in 1016. He ruled England for
nineteen years. The story goes that his fawning admirers told him that he was
a god and could even turn back the tides. He showed them he couldn't, that
he was as mortal as them. He is remembered as a wise and successful king of
England who united Britain.

THE THROWING-HORSESHOES WORLD CUP
(A sporting tale from the Dark Ages)

I could have been an archer
And I'm pretty good at tag
I could have been a swimmer in the lake
At dancing I'm not bad
But I'm not as good as Dad
My skill is throwing horseshoes at a stake

Don't get in a fight with Ulric
He's a boxer, and he's good
And Merek walks on stilts full two yards high
Playing rugby? I would say
Don't get in Mary's way
But for horseshoe throwing, I'm the come-to guy

One day my fame will spread
From Muggleswick to Penny Pie
And songs will be sung and tales made up
How Leofrick of Slough
In a thousand years from now
Will be the first name on the Horseshoe World Cup

Roger Stevens

> *When you mention sport in the Dark Ages most people think of jousting. But in this period stirrups hadn't been adopted in Europe, and so staying on a horse would have been almost impossible in a joust. And although there's no Throwing-Horseshoes World Cup, horseshoe pitching is still a popular game in the USA.*

AFTER THE ROMANS

THE GREAT KING ALFRED

As the Danes tried to conquer
And settle in these lands
The importance of King Alfred's legacy
Cannot be overstated
He united a country of kingdoms
In a right royal mess
I'd tell you how he sorted it,
But it's much too complicated.

Roger Stevens

It really was very complicated. To find out more you'll need to look in some history books or search the internet.

KING ALFRED AND THE CAKES

King Alfred was great: he established schools, gave
    us laws and he rarely, well, seldom
Made mistakes
Until, whilst staying unrecognized at a peasant's
    house, he was asked to watch the stove and while
    his mind was on the Danes he
Burnt the cakes
The woman she was cross and told him off, then said,
    It's nearly suppertime – don't
Burn the gravy
What happened to the peasant present history does
    not tell, but King Alfred left to found the
Royal Navy

Roger Stevens

AFTER THE ROMANS

THE PROPHECY OF LOVE

The birth of the Prophet Muhammad
The prophecy of love
From the pinhole camera
To mariner's compass
From Islamic architecture
To Urdu literature
Such were the fruits of this religion
How important, He said
To make peace between one another
Enmity and malice, He said,
Tear up heavenly rewards
By the roots

Roger Stevens

The birth of Prophet Muhammad in 570 CE had a profound effect on world history, setting the stage for the Italian Renaissance and ultimately the Crusades.

A SHORT HISTORY OF RELIGION

In the old, old days
There were so many gods
There was a god for just about anything
A god of the sun
A god to send rain
A god for love and happiness
A god of misery and pain

In Egypt, so many gods
Hathor, the goddess of love
Ra, the god of the sun,
Khonsu, the god of the moon
Heket, the goddess of frogs
Babi, the god of baboons

In Greece, so many gods . . .
Hemera, the goddess of day
Nyx, the goddess of night
Aphrodite was the goddess of love
Aether, the god of light

AFTER THE ROMANS

In Rome, so many gods
And some they copied from the Greeks
Venus, the goddess of love
Bacchus, the god of brewers
They even had a goddess called Cloacina
Goddess of the sewers

The Vikings, so many gods
Freya, the goddess of love
Ullr, the god of skis
Loki, the god of mischief
Víðarr, the god of silence and revenge
And trees

But the Jewish people
Had only one God
And from that religion was born
Christianity
And Muslims also
Worship that same one God

And so wouldn't you think
That the Jews and Christians and Muslims
Would be the best of friends?

Roger Stevens

AFTER THE ROMANS

THE PLOUGHMAN

The thatcher mends roofs with straw or reeds.
The priest looks after our spiritual needs.
The swordsman keeps our enemies at bay
but the ploughman slices the clay.

The fisherman fishes with net, bait and hook.
The teacher reads God's words from His book.
The seamstress stitches clothes by hand
but the ploughman tills the land.

The merchant brings us cloth and silk.
The herdsman supplies our daily milk.
The blacksmith works with iron and lead
but the ploughman gives us bread.

The farmer grows apples, berries and sloes.
The shoemaker fashions leather shoes.
The labourer mends a broken wall
but the ploughman feeds us all.

Brian Moses

'The ploughman feeds us well,' declared Aelfric, a Wessex schoolmaster, c.1000 CE.

AFTER THE ROMANS

HAROLD & WILLIAM & 1066

Hastings was harder for Harold
after Harald Hardrada was routed at York,
even though Hastings was a 'home match'
and it should have been easier.

It was the long march north followed by
the long march south that did for his army.
It was slog upon slog, footsore and aching,
dog-tired, mired in mud, no time
for rest and recuperation.

William, of course, was scouting around in Sussex,
trampling down crops and annoying the locals.
Pretty vocal too, with his threats about
what he would do to the Brits if they thwarted him.
He had ample time to prepare for the fight,
to check out the lie of the land and decide
where his cavalry would best be stationed.

Strangely enough though, Harold could have won.
His army had a good position on top of a hill
and Norman arrows rained harmlessly down
on their shields. But William was a teaser
who pretended to retreat, made out his troops were
    beat,
till Harold's men broke ranks, left the hill
and were easily killed by the cavalry.

Who knows what really befell Harold?
An arrow in the eye sounds a strange way to die.
More likely he was struck down while blinded.

Quelle catastrophe pour les Anglais,
what a blow to national pride.
Still strange to think that the date we all know
was a lost battle, fought at huge cost.

Brian Moses

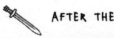

AFTER THE ROMANS

BATTLEFIELD

This place could be
the battlefield.

This could be the place
where Harold's army,
tired and footsore,
stood their ground
as William's army
bore down on them.

And it isn't hard to imagine
the ranting and roaring,
the flutter of pennants,
the pounding of hoofs,
the clashing of swords,
and the frightened steeds
trampling warriors.

And then when it seemed
the battle might be won,
William's army feigned retreat.
History records how a shower
of arrows fired in the air
left Harold dying, his troops
leaderless.

It was all so long ago,
so many memories in the mist,
so many summers, frozen winters.
Who really cares if it was fought
elsewhere?

Yet I hear it still,
down the ages, drawn like the wind
in the wires.

But who will hear it
in years to come,
buried beneath layers of earth,
silenced by the thunder of wheels?

Brian Moses

There are different opinions these days as to where the Battle of Hastings actually took place. One opinion is that it was fought where a road and a roundabout now stand.

 AFTER THE ROMANS

What Are We Fighting For?

Brian Moses and Roger Stevens

Fascinating and moving in equal measure, this brand-new collection of poetry from Brian Moses and Roger Stevens explores the topic of war in a brilliantly accessible way for younger readers.

Find out about incredibly brave animals on the battlefield, the day soldiers played football in no-man's-land, poems about rationing and what it was like to be an evacuee, plus poems about the idea of warfare, asking the question What Are We Fighting For?

NEW POEMS ABOUT WAR

WWW.GOBSTOPPERBOOKS.COM

VISIT THE GOBSTOPPERS WEBSITE FOR

AUTHOR NEWS · BONUS CONTENT
VIDEOS · GAMES · PRIZES . . .
AND MORE!

MACMILLAN
Children's Books